MICHAEL JACKSON
Instrumental Solos

Arranged by BILL GALLIFORD, ETHAN NEUBURG and TOD EDMONDSON

Produced by
Alfred Music Publishing Co., Inc.
P.O. Box 10003
Van Nuys, CA 91410-0003
alfred.com

Printed in USA.

ISBN-10: 0-7390-7795-3
ISBN-13: 978-0-7390-7795-5

CONTENTS

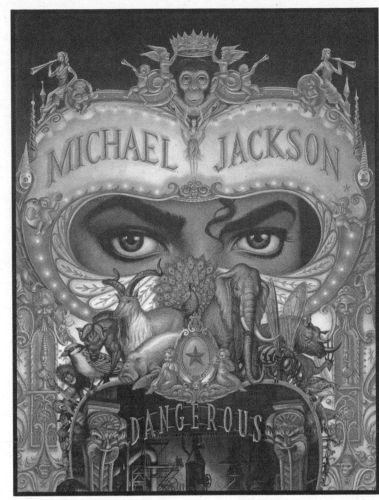

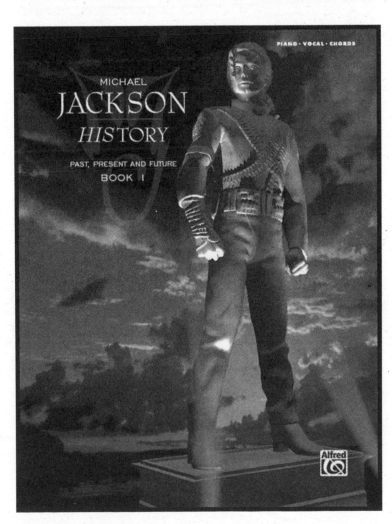

Track 2: Demo
Track 3: Play Along

BEAT IT

Written and Composed by
MICHAEL JACKSON

Moderately fast ♩ = 138

9 *Verse:*

mf

17

25 *Chorus:*

f

BILLIE JEAN

Track 4: Demo
Track 5: Play Along

Written and Composed by
MICHAEL JACKSON

Moderately ♩ = 116

Verse:

mf

Billie Jean - 2 - 1

8

BLACK OR WHITE

Rap Lyrics Written by
BILL BOTTRELL

Written and Composed by
MICHAEL JACKSON

Track 6: Demo
Track 7: Play Along

Moderate funk ♩ = 116

33 *Optional Rap:*

(Spoken:) Protection for gangs, clubs, and nations,   *causing grief in human relations.*

Black or White - 2 - 1

It's a turf war,   *on a global scale.*   *I'd rather hear both sides of the tale.*

You see, it's not about races, just places,   *faces. Where your blood comes from is where your space is.*

I've seen the sharp get duller,   *I'm not going to spend my life being a color.*

DON'T STOP 'TIL YOU GET ENOUGH

Track 8: Demo
Track 9: Play Along

Written and Composed by
MICHAEL JACKSON

Moderate dance tempo ♩ = 112

Verse:

Don't Stop 'til You Get Enough - 2 - 1

HUMAN NATURE

Track 10: Demo
Track 11: Play Along

Words and Music by
JOHN BETTIS and JEFF PORCARO

Human Nature - 2 - 1

I JUST CAN'T STOP LOVING YOU

Track 12: Demo
Track 13: Play Along

Written and Composed by
MICHAEL JACKSON

Moderately (♩ = 100) *Verse:*

I Just Can't Stop Loving You - 2 - 1

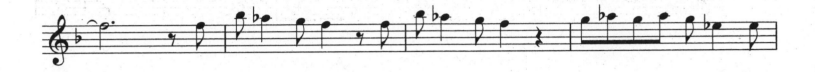

Chorus:

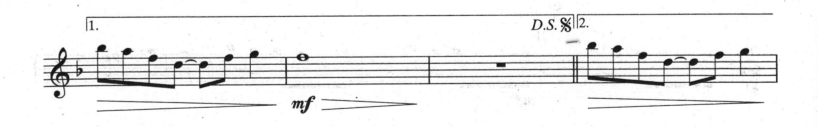

I Just Can't Stop Loving You - 2 - 2

THE WAY YOU MAKE ME FEEL

Track 14: Demo
Track 15: Play Along

Written and Composed by
MICHAEL JACKSON

The Way You Make Me Feel - 2 - 1

To Coda ⊕

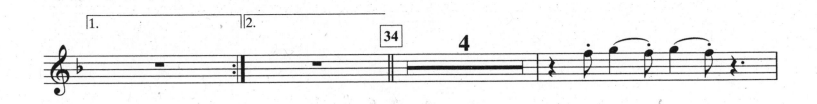

D.S. 𝄋 *al Coda*

⊕ *Coda*

The Way You Make Me Feel - 2 - 2

SHE'S OUT OF MY LIFE

Track 16: Demo
Track 17: Play Along

Words and Music by
TOM BAHLER

Slowly, with expression (♩ = 72)

She's Out of My Life - 2 - 1

Track 18: Demo
Track 19: Play Along

WILL YOU BE THERE

Written and Composed by
MICHAEL JACKSON

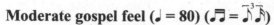

Moderate gospel feel (♩ = 80)

Verse:
legato

mp – mf

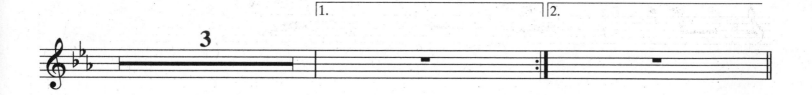

Bridge:

Will You Be There - 2 - 1

Verse:

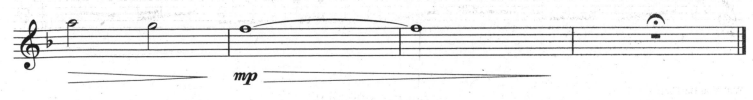

MAN IN THE MIRROR

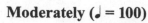

Track 20: Demo
Track 21: Play Along

Words and Music by
SIEDAH GARRETT and GLEN BALLARD

Moderately (♩ = 100)

Man in the Mirror - 2 - 1

THRILLER

Track 22: Demo
Track 23: Play Along

Words and Music by
ROD TEMPERTON

Thriller - 2 - 2

Track 24: Demo
Track 25: Play Along

YOU ARE NOT ALONE

Words and Music by
R. KELLY

You Are Not Alone - 2 - 1

31 *Chorus:*

39

rit. *mf*

PARTS OF A FLUTE AND FINGERING CHART

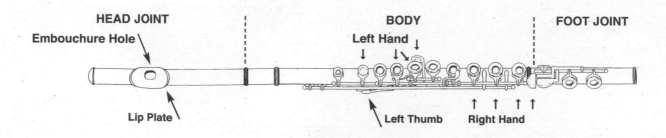

● = press the key.
○ = do not press the key.

When there are two fingerings given for a note, use the first one unless the
alternate fingering is suggested.

When two enharmonic notes are given together (F♯ and G♭ as an example), they sound
the same pitch and are played the same way.